United States of America v.
Donald J. Trump and Waltine Nauta

The complete indictment including color photos from Mar-a-Lago

Welcome Rain Publishers
New York

Please NOTE: This is not a publication of the United States Government

The United States of America v. Donald J. Trump and Waltine Nauta

Cover copyright © 2023 Welcome Rain Publishers (LLC)
Cover photo and photos on pages 12, 14, and 20 provided by The Associated Press.
Photos on pages 15 and 16 provided by Getty Images News.

Designed by Laura Smyth, Smythtype Design

10 9 8 7 6 5 4 3 2 1
Library of Congress Cataloging in Publication Data is available from the publisher.
Direct any inquiries to Welcome Rain Publishers LLC.

Printed in the USA
ISBN 978-1-56649-430-4

UNITED STATES DISTRICT COURT
SOUTHERN DISTRICT OF FLORIDA

23-80101-CR-CANNON/REINHART

Case No. _____

18 U.S.C. § 793(e)
18 U.S.C. § 1512(k)
18 U.S.C. § 1512(b)(2)(A)
18 U.S.C. § 1512(c)(1)
18 U.S.C. § 1519
18 U.S.C. § 1001(a)(1)
18 U.S.C. § 1001(a)(2)
18 U.S.C. § 2

UNITED STATES OF AMERICA

v.

DONALD J. TRUMP and
WALTINE NAUTA,

      Defendants.

_____/

INDICTMENT

The Grand Jury charges that:

GENERAL ALLEGATIONS

At times material to this Indictment, on or about the dates and approximate times stated below:

Introduction

1.   Defendant **DONALD J. TRUMP** was the forty-fifth President of the United States of America. He held office from January 20, 2017, until January 20, 2021. As president, **TRUMP** had lawful access to the most sensitive classified documents and national defense information gathered and owned by the United States government, including information from the agencies that comprise the United States Intelligence Community and the United States Department of Defense.

2.   Over the course of his presidency, **TRUMP** gathered newspapers, press clippings, letters, notes, cards, photographs, official documents, and other materials in cardboard boxes that he kept in the White House. Among the materials **TRUMP** stored in his boxes were hundreds of classified documents.

3.   The classified documents **TRUMP** stored in his boxes included information regarding defense and weapons capabilities of both the United States and foreign countries; United States nuclear programs; potential vulnerabilities of the United States and its allies to military attack; and plans for possible retaliation in response to a foreign attack. The unauthorized disclosure of these classified documents could put at risk the national security of the United States, foreign relations, the safety of the United States military, and human sources and the continued viability of sensitive intelligence collection methods.

4.   At 12:00 p.m. on January 20, 2021, **TRUMP** ceased to be president. As he departed the White House, **TRUMP** caused scores of boxes, many of which contained classified documents, to be transported to The Mar-a-Lago Club in Palm Beach, Florida, where he maintained his residence. **TRUMP** was not authorized to possess or retain those classified documents.

5.   The Mar-a-Lago Club was an active social club, which, between January 2021 and August 2022, hosted events for tens of thousands of members and guests. After **TRUMP**'s presidency, The Mar-a-Lago Club was not an authorized location for the storage, possession, review, display, or discussion of classified documents. Nevertheless, **TRUMP** stored his boxes containing classified documents in various locations at The Mar-a-Lago Club—including in a ballroom, a bathroom and shower, an office space, his bedroom, and a storage room.

6.   On two occasions in 2021, **TRUMP** showed classified documents to others, as follows:

a. In July 2021, at Trump National Golf Club in Bedminster, New Jersey ("The Bedminster Club"), during an audio-recorded meeting with a writer, a publisher, and two members of his staff, none of whom possessed a security clearance, **TRUMP** showed and described a "plan of attack" that **TRUMP** said was prepared for him by the Department of Defense and a senior military official. **TRUMP** told the individuals that the plan was "highly confidential" and "secret." **TRUMP** also said, "as president I could have declassified it," and, "Now I can't, you know, but this is still a secret."

b. In August or September 2021, at The Bedminster Club, **TRUMP** showed a representative of his political action committee who did not possess a security clearance a classified map related to a military operation and told the representative that he should not be showing it to the representative and that the representative should not get too close.

7. On March 30, 2022, the Federal Bureau of Investigation ("FBI") opened a criminal investigation into the unlawful retention of classified documents at The Mar-a-Lago Club. A federal grand jury investigation began the next month. The grand jury issued a subpoena requiring **TRUMP** to turn over all documents with classification markings. **TRUMP** endeavored to obstruct the FBI and grand jury investigations and conceal his continued retention of classified documents by, among other things:

a. suggesting that his attorney falsely represent to the FBI and grand jury that **TRUMP** did not have documents called for by the grand jury subpoena;

b. directing defendant **WALTINE NAUTA** to move boxes of documents to conceal them from **TRUMP**'s attorney, the FBI, and the grand jury;

c. suggesting that his attorney hide or destroy documents called for by the grand jury subpoena;

d. providing to the FBI and grand jury just some of the documents called for by the grand jury subpoena, while claiming that he was cooperating fully; and

e. causing a certification to be submitted to the FBI and grand jury falsely representing that all documents called for by the grand jury subpoena had been produced—while knowing that, in fact, not all such documents had been produced.

8.   As a result of **TRUMP**'s retention of classified documents after his presidency and refusal to return them, hundreds of classified documents were not recovered by the United States government until 2022, as follows:

    a.   On January 17, nearly one year after **TRUMP** left office, and after months of demands by the National Archives and Records Administration for **TRUMP** to provide all missing presidential records, **TRUMP** provided only 15 boxes, which contained 197 documents with classification markings.

    b.   On June 3, in response to a grand jury subpoena demanding the production of all documents with classification markings, **TRUMP**'s attorney provided to the FBI 38 more documents with classification markings.

    c.   On August 8, pursuant to a court-authorized search warrant, the FBI recovered from **TRUMP**'s office and a storage room at The Mar-a-Lago Club 102 more documents with classification markings.

TRUMP's Co-Conspirator

9.   Defendant **NAUTA** was a member of the United States Navy stationed as a valet in the White House during **TRUMP**'s presidency. Beginning in August 2021, **NAUTA** became an executive assistant in The Office of Donald J. Trump and served as **TRUMP**'s personal aide or "body man." **NAUTA** reported to **TRUMP**, worked closely with **TRUMP**, and traveled with **TRUMP**.

The Mar-a-Lago Club

10.   The Mar-a-Lago Club was located on South Ocean Boulevard in Palm Beach, Florida, and included **TRUMP**'s residence, more than 25 guest rooms, two ballrooms, a spa, a gift store, exercise facilities, office space, and an outdoor pool and patio. As of January 2021, The Mar-a-Lago Club had hundreds of members and was staffed by more than 150 full-time, part-time, and temporary employees.

11.   Between January 2021 and August 2022, The Mar-a-Lago Club hosted more than 150 social events, including weddings, movie premieres, and fundraisers that together drew tens of thousands of guests.

12.   The United States Secret Service (the "Secret Service") provided protection services to **TRUMP** and his family after he left office, including at The Mar-a-Lago Club, but it was not responsible for the protection of **TRUMP**'s boxes or their contents. **TRUMP** did not inform the Secret Service that he was storing boxes containing classified documents at The Mar-a-Lago Club.

Classified Information

13.   National security information was information owned by, produced by, produced for, and under the control of the United States government. Pursuant to Executive Order 12958, signed on April 17, 1995, as amended by Executive Order 13292 on March 25, 2003, and Executive Order 13526 on December 29, 2009, national security information was classified as "TOP SECRET," "SECRET," or "CONFIDENTIAL," as follows:

  a.   Information was classified as TOP SECRET if the unauthorized disclosure of that information reasonably could be expected to cause exceptionally grave damage to the national security that the original classification authority was able to identify or describe.

  b.   Information was classified as SECRET if the unauthorized disclosure of that information reasonably could be expected to cause serious damage to the national security that the original classification authority was able to identify or describe.

  c.   Information was classified as CONFIDENTIAL if the unauthorized disclosure of that information reasonably could be expected to cause damage to the national security that the original classification authority was able to identify or describe.

14.   The classification marking "NOFORN" stood for "Not Releasable to Foreign Nationals" and denoted that dissemination of that information was limited to United States persons.

15.   Classified information related to intelligence sources, methods, and analytical processes was designated as Sensitive Compartmented Information ("SCI"). SCI was to be processed, stored, used, or discussed in an accredited Sensitive Compartmented Information Facility ("SCIF"), and only individuals with the appropriate security clearance and additional SCI permissions were authorized to have access to such national security information.

16.   When the vulnerability of, or threat to, specific classified information was exceptional, and the normal criteria for determining eligibility for access to classified information were insufficient to protect the information from unauthorized disclosure, the United States could establish Special Access Programs ("SAPs") to further protect the classified information. The number of these programs was to be kept to an absolute minimum and limited to programs in which the number of persons who ordinarily would have access would be reasonably small and commensurate with the objective of providing enhanced protection for the information involved. Only individuals with the appropriate security clearance and additional SAP permissions were authorized to have access to such national security information, which was subject to enhanced handling and storage requirements.

17.   Pursuant to Executive Order 13526, information classified at any level could be lawfully accessed only by persons determined by an appropriate United States government official to be eligible for access to classified information and who had signed an approved non-disclosure agreement, who received a security clearance, and who had a "need-to-know" the classified

information. After his presidency, **TRUMP** was not authorized to possess or retain classified documents.

18.   Executive Order 13526 provided that a former president could obtain a waiver of the "need-to-know" requirement, if the agency head or senior agency official of the agency that originated the classified information: (1) determined in writing that access was consistent with the interest of national security and (2) took appropriate steps to protect classified information from unauthorized disclosure or compromise and ensured that the information was safeguarded in a manner consistent with the order. **TRUMP** did not obtain any such waiver after his presidency.

The Executive Branch Departments and Agencies Whose Classified Documents TRUMP Retained After His Presidency

19.   As part of his official duties as president, **TRUMP** received intelligence briefings from high-level United States government officials, including briefings from the Director of the Central Intelligence Agency, the Chairman of the Joint Chiefs of Staff, senior White House officials, and a designated briefer. He regularly received a collection of classified intelligence from the United States Intelligence Community ("USIC") known as the "President's Daily Brief."

20.   The USIC's mission was to collect, analyze, and deliver foreign intelligence and counterintelligence information to America's leaders, including the president, policymakers, law enforcement, and the military, so they could make sound decisions to protect the United States. The USIC consisted of United States executive branch departments and agencies responsible for the conduct of foreign relations and the protection of national security.

21.   After his presidency, **TRUMP** retained classified documents originated by, or implicating the equities of, multiple USIC members and other executive branch departments and agencies, including the following:

a.   **The Central Intelligence Agency ("CIA").** CIA was responsible for providing intelligence on foreign countries and global issues to the president and other policymakers to help them make national security decisions.

b.   **The Department of Defense ("DoD").** DoD was responsible for providing the military forces needed to deter war and ensure national security. Some of the executive branch agencies comprising the USIC were within DoD.

c.   **The National Security Agency.** The National Security Agency was a combat support agency within DoD and a member of the USIC responsible for foreign signals intelligence and cybersecurity. This included collecting, processing, and disseminating to United States policymakers and military leaders foreign intelligence derived from communications and information systems; protecting national security systems; and enabling computer network operations.

d.   **The National Geospatial Intelligence Agency.** The National Geospatial Intelligence Agency was a combat support agency within DoD responsible for the exploitation and analysis of imagery, imagery intelligence, and geospatial information in support of the national security objectives of the United States and the geospatial intelligence requirements of DoD, the Department of State, and other federal agencies.

e.   **The National Reconnaissance Office.** The National Reconnaissance Office was an agency within DoD responsible for developing, acquiring, launching, and operating space-based surveillance and reconnaissance systems that collected and delivered intelligence to enhance national security.

f.   **The Department of Energy.** The Department of Energy was responsible for maintaining a safe, secure, and effective nuclear deterrent to protect national security, including ensuring the effectiveness of the United States nuclear weapons stockpile without nuclear explosive testing.

g.   **The Department of State and Bureau of Intelligence and Research.** The Department of State was responsible for protecting and promoting United States security, prosperity, and democratic values. Within the Department of State, the Bureau of Intelligence and Research was a member of the USIC and responsible for providing intelligence to inform diplomacy and support United States diplomats.

TRUMP's Public Statements on Classified Information

22.   As a candidate for President of the United States, **TRUMP** made the following public statements, among others, about classified information:

   a.   On August 18, 2016, **TRUMP** stated, "In my administration I'm going to enforce all laws concerning the protection of classified information. No one will be above the law."

   b.   On September 6, 2016, **TRUMP** stated, "We also need to fight this battle by collecting intelligence and then protecting, protecting our classified secrets. . . . We can't have someone in the Oval Office who doesn't understand the meaning of the word confidential or classified."

   c.   On September 7, 2016, **TRUMP** stated, "[O]ne of the first things we must do is to enforce all classification rules and to enforce all laws relating to the handling of classified information."

   d.   On September 19, 2016, **TRUMP** stated, "We also need the best protection of classified information."

   e.   On November 3, 2016, **TRUMP** stated, "Service members here in North Carolina have risked their lives to acquire classified intelligence to protect our country."

23.   As President of the United States, on July 26, 2018, **TRUMP** issued the following statement about classified information:

> As the head of the executive branch and Commander in Chief, I have a unique, Constitutional responsibility to protect the Nation's classified information, including by controlling access to it. . . . More broadly, the issue of [a former executive branch official's] security clearance raises larger questions about the practice of former officials maintaining access to our Nation's most sensitive secrets long after their time in Government has ended. Such access is particularly inappropriate when former officials have transitioned into highly partisan positions and seek to use real or perceived access to sensitive information to validate their political attacks. Any access granted to our Nation's secrets should be in furtherance of national, not personal, interests.

TRUMP's Retention of Classified Documents After His Presidency

24.   In January 2021, as he was preparing to leave the White House, **TRUMP** and his White House staff, including **NAUTA**, packed items, including some of **TRUMP**'s boxes. **TRUMP** was personally involved in this process. **TRUMP** caused his boxes, containing hundreds of classified documents, to be transported from the White House to The Mar-a-Lago Club.

25.   From January through March 15, 2021, some of **TRUMP**'s boxes were stored in The Mar-a-Lago Club's White and Gold Ballroom, in which events and gatherings took place. **TRUMP**'s boxes were for a time stacked on the ballroom's stage, as depicted in the photograph below (redacted to obscure an individual's identity).

26.   In March 2021, **NAUTA** and others moved some of **TRUMP**'s boxes from the White and Gold Ballroom to the business center at The Mar-a-Lago Club.

27.   On April 5, 2021, an employee of The Office of Donald J. Trump ("Trump Employee 1") texted another employee of that office ("Trump Employee 2") to ask whether **TRUMP**'s boxes could be moved out of the business center to make room for staff to use it as an office. Trump Employee 2 replied, "Woah!! Ok so potus specifically asked Walt for those boxes to be in the business center because they are his 'papers.'" Later that day, Trump Employee 1 and Trump Employee 2 exchanged the following text messages:

> Trump Employee 2:
>
>> We can definitely make it work if we move his papers into the lake room?
>
> Trump Employee 1:
>
>> There is still a little room in the shower where his other stuff is. Is it only his papers he cares about? Theres some other stuff in there that are not papers. Could that go to storage? Or does he want everything in there on property
>
> Trump Employee 2:
>
>> Yes - anything that's not the beautiful mind paper boxes can definitely go to storage. Want to take a look at the space and start moving tomorrow AM?

28.   After the text exchange between Trump Employee 1 and Trump Employee 2, in April 2021, some of **TRUMP**'s boxes were moved from the business center to a bathroom and shower in The Mar-a-Lago Club's Lake Room, as depicted in the photograph below.

29. In May 2021, **TRUMP** directed that a storage room on the ground floor of The Mar-a-Lago Club (the "Storage Room") be cleaned out so that it could be used to store his boxes. The hallway leading to the Storage Room could be reached from multiple outside entrances, including one accessible from The Mar-a-Lago Club pool patio through a doorway that was often kept open. The Storage Room was near the liquor supply closet, linen room, lock shop, and various other rooms.

30. On June 24, 2021, **TRUMP**'s boxes that were in the Lake Room were moved to the Storage Room. After the move, there were more than 80 boxes in the Storage Room, as depicted in the photographs below.

31.   On December 7, 2021, **NAUTA** found several of **TRUMP**'s boxes fallen and their

contents spilled onto the floor of the Storage Room, including a document marked "SECRET//REL

TO USA, FVEY," which denoted that the information in the document was releasable only to the Five Eyes intelligence alliance consisting of Australia, Canada, New Zealand, the United Kingdom, and the United States. **NAUTA** texted Trump Employee 2, "I opened the door and found this…" **NAUTA** also attached two photographs he took of the spill. Trump Employee 2 replied, "Oh no oh no," and "I'm sorry potus had my phone." One of the photographs **NAUTA** texted to Trump Employee 2 is depicted below with the visible classified information redacted. **TRUMP**'s unlawful retention of this document is charged in Count 8 of this Indictment.

TRUMP's Disclosures of Classified Information in Private Meetings

32.   In May 2021, **TRUMP** caused some of his boxes to be brought to his summer residence at The Bedminster Club. Like The Mar-a-Lago Club, after **TRUMP**'s presidency, The Bedminster Club was not an authorized location for the storage, possession, review, display, or discussion of classified documents.

33.   On July 21, 2021, when he was no longer president, **TRUMP** gave an interview in his office at The Bedminster Club to a writer and a publisher in connection with a then-forthcoming book. Two members of **TRUMP**'s staff also attended the interview, which was recorded with **TRUMP**'s knowledge and consent. Before the interview, the media had published reports that, at the end of **TRUMP**'s term as president, a senior military official (the "Senior Military Official") purportedly feared that **TRUMP** might order an attack on Country A and that the Senior Military Official advised **TRUMP** against doing so.

34.   Upon greeting the writer, publisher, and his two staff members, **TRUMP** stated, "Look what I found, this was [the Senior Military Official's] plan of attack, read it and just show . . . it's interesting." Later in the interview, **TRUMP** engaged in the following exchange:

TRUMP:	Well, with [the Senior Military Official]—uh, let me see that, I'll show you an example. He said that I wanted to attack [Country A]. Isn't it amazing? I have a big pile of papers, this thing just came up. Look. This was him. They presented me this—this is off the record, but—they presented me this. This was him. This was the Defense Department and him.
WRITER:	Wow.
TRUMP:	We looked at some. This was him. This wasn't done by me, this was him. All sorts of stuff—pages long, look.
STAFFER:	Mm.
TRUMP:	Wait a minute, let's see here.
STAFFER:	*[Laughter]* Yeah.
TRUMP:	I just found, isn't that amazing? This totally wins my case, you know.
STAFFER:	Mm-hm.
TRUMP:	Except it is like, highly confidential.

STAFFER:	Yeah. *[Laughter]*
TRUMP:	Secret. This is secret information. Look, look at this. You attack, and—

* * *

TRUMP:	By the way. Isn't that incredible?
STAFFER:	Yeah.
TRUMP:	I was just thinking, because we were talking about it. And you know, he said, "he wanted to attack [Country A], and what . . ."
STAFFER:	You did.
TRUMP:	This was done by the military and given to me. Uh, I think we can probably, right?
STAFFER:	I don't know, we'll, we'll have to see. Yeah, we'll have to try to—
TRUMP:	Declassify it.
STAFFER:	—figure out a—yeah.
TRUMP:	See as president I could have declassified it.
STAFFER:	Yeah. *[Laughter]*
TRUMP:	Now I can't, you know, but this is still a secret.
STAFFER:	Yeah. *[Laughter]* Now we have a problem.
TRUMP:	Isn't that interesting?

At the time of this exchange, the writer, the publisher, and **TRUMP**'s two staff members did not have security clearances or any need-to-know any classified information about a plan of attack on Country A.

35.   In August or September 2021, when he was no longer president, **TRUMP** met in his office at The Bedminster Club with a representative of his political action committee (the "PAC

Representative"). During the meeting, **TRUMP** commented that an ongoing military operation in Country B was not going well. **TRUMP** showed the PAC Representative a classified map of Country B and told the PAC Representative that he should not be showing the map to the PAC Representative and to not get too close. The PAC Representative did not have a security clearance or any need-to-know classified information about the military operation.

36. On February 16, 2017, four years before **TRUMP**'s disclosures of classified information set forth above, **TRUMP** said at a press conference:

> The first thing I thought of when I heard about it is, how does the press get this information that's classified? How do they do it? You know why? Because it's an illegal process, and the press should be ashamed of themselves. But more importantly, the people that gave out the information to the press should be ashamed of themselves. Really ashamed.

TRUMP's Production of 15 Cardboard Boxes to the National Archives and Records Administration

37. Beginning in May 2021, the National Archives and Records Administration ("NARA"), which was responsible for archiving presidential records, repeatedly demanded that **TRUMP** turn over presidential records that he had kept after his presidency. On multiple occasions, beginning in June, NARA warned **TRUMP** through his representatives that if he did not comply, it would refer the matter of the missing records to the Department of Justice.

38. Between November 2021 and January 2022, **NAUTA** and Trump Employee 2—at **TRUMP**'s direction—brought boxes from the Storage Room to **TRUMP**'s residence for **TRUMP** to review.

39. On November 12, 2021, Trump Employee 2 provided **TRUMP** a photograph of his boxes in the Storage Room by taping it to one of the boxes that Trump Employee 2 had placed in **TRUMP**'s residence. Trump Employee 2 provided **TRUMP** the photograph so that **TRUMP**

could see how many of his boxes were stored in the Storage Room. The photograph, shown below, depicted a wall of the Storage Room against which dozens of **TRUMP**'s boxes were stacked.

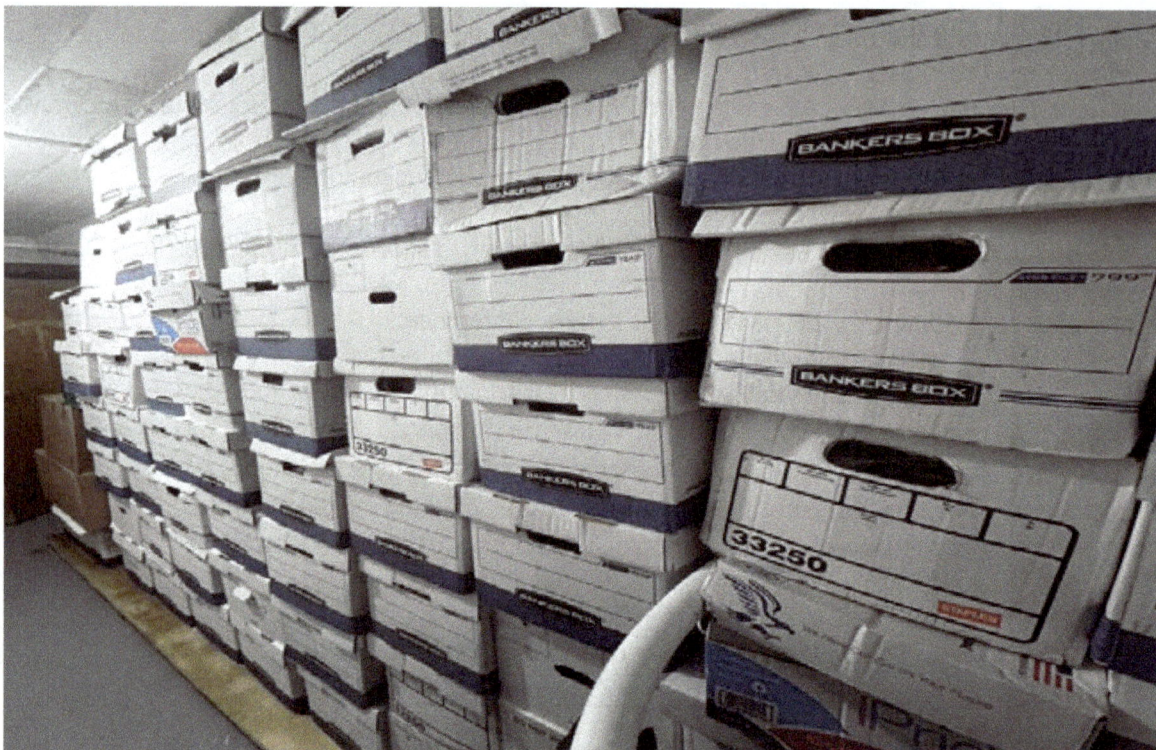

40.   On November 17, 2021, **NAUTA** texted Trump Employee 2 about the photograph Trump Employee 2 had provided to **TRUMP**, stating, "He mentioned about a picture of the 'boxes' he wants me to see it?" Trump Employee 2 replied, "Calling you shortly."

41.   On November 25, 2021, Trump Employee 2 texted **NAUTA** about **TRUMP**'s review of the contents of his boxes, asking, "Has he mentioned boxes to you? I delivered some, but I think he may need more. Could you ask if he'd like more in pine hall?" Pine Hall was an entry room in **TRUMP**'s residence. **NAUTA** replied in three successive text messages:

> Nothing about boxes yet
>
> He has one he's working on in pine hall
>
> Knocked out 2 boxes yesterday

42.   On November 29, 2021, Trump Employee 2 texted **NAUTA**, asking, "Next you are on property (no rush) could you help me bring 4 more boxes up?" **NAUTA** replied, "Yes!! Of course."

43.   On December 29, 2021, Trump Employee 2 texted a **TRUMP** representative who was in contact with NARA ("Trump Representative 1"), "box answer will be wrenched out of him today, promise!" The next day, Trump Representative 1 replied in two successive text messages:

Hey - Just checking on Boxes…

would love to have a number to them today

Trump Employee 2 spoke to **TRUMP** and then responded a few hours later in two successive text messages:

12

Is his number

44.   On January 13, 2022, **NAUTA** texted Trump Employee 2 about **TRUMP**'s "tracking" of boxes, stating, "He's tracking the boxes, more to follow today on whether he wants to go through more today or tomorrow." Trump Employee 2 replied, "Thank you!"

45.   On January 15, 2022, **NAUTA** sent Trump Employee 2 four successive text messages:

One thing he asked

Was for new covers for the boxes, for Monday m.

Morning

*can we get new box covers before giving these to them on Monday? They have too much writing on them..I marked too much

Trump Employee 2 replied, "Yes, I will get that!"

46.   On January 17, 2022, Trump Employee 2 and **NAUTA** gathered 15 boxes from **TRUMP**'s residence, loaded the boxes in **NAUTA**'s car, and took them to a commercial truck for delivery to NARA.

47.   When interviewed by the FBI in May 2022 regarding the location and movement of boxes before the production to NARA, **NAUTA** made false and misleading statements as set forth in Count 38 of this Indictment, including:

a.   falsely stating that he was not aware of **TRUMP**'s boxes being brought to **TRUMP**'s residence for his review before **TRUMP** provided 15 boxes to NARA in January 2022;

b.   falsely stating that he did not know how the boxes that he and Trump Employee 2 brought from **TRUMP**'s residence to the commercial truck for delivery to NARA on January 17, 2022, had gotten to the residence; and

c.   when asked whether he knew where **TRUMP**'s boxes had been stored before they were in **TRUMP**'s residence and whether they had been in a secure or locked location, **NAUTA** falsely responded, "I wish, I wish I could tell you. I don't know. I don't—I honestly just don't know."

48.   When the 15 boxes that **TRUMP** had provided reached NARA in January 2022, NARA reviewed the contents and determined that 14 of the boxes contained documents with classification markings. Specifically, as the FBI later determined, the boxes contained 197 documents with classification markings, of which 98 were marked "SECRET," 30 were marked "TOP SECRET," and the remainder were marked "CONFIDENTIAL." Some of those documents also contained SCI and SAP markings.

49.   On February 9, 2022, NARA referred the discovery of classified documents in **TRUMP**'s boxes to the Department of Justice for investigation.

The FBI and Grand Jury Investigations

50.   On March 30, 2022, the FBI opened a criminal investigation.

51.   On April 26, 2022, a federal grand jury opened an investigation.

The Defendants' Concealment of Boxes

52.   On May 11, 2022, the grand jury issued a subpoena (the "May 11 Subpoena") to The Office of Donald J. Trump requiring the production of all documents with classification markings in the possession, custody, or control of **TRUMP** or The Office of Donald J. Trump. Two attorneys representing **TRUMP** ("Trump Attorney 1" and "Trump Attorney 2") informed **TRUMP** of the May 11 Subpoena, and he authorized Trump Attorney 1 to accept service.

53.   On May 22, 2022, **NAUTA** entered the Storage Room at 3:47 p.m. and left approximately 34 minutes later, carrying one of **TRUMP**'s boxes.

54.   On May 23, 2022, **TRUMP** met with Trump Attorney 1 and Trump Attorney 2 at The Mar-a-Lago Club to discuss the response to the May 11 Subpoena. Trump Attorney 1 and Trump Attorney 2 told **TRUMP** that they needed to search for documents that would be responsive to the subpoena and provide a certification that there had been compliance with the subpoena. **TRUMP**, in sum and substance, made the following statements, among others, as memorialized by Trump Attorney 1:

> a.   I don't want anybody looking, I don't want anybody looking through my boxes, I really don't, I don't want you looking through my boxes.
>
> b.   Well what if we, what happens if we just don't respond at all or don't play ball with them?
>
> c.   Wouldn't it be better if we just told them we don't have anything here?
>
> d.   Well look isn't it better if there are no documents?

55.   While meeting with Trump Attorney 1 and Trump Attorney 2 on May 23, **TRUMP**, in sum and substance, told the following story, as memorialized by Trump Attorney 1:

> [Attorney], he was great, he did a great job. You know what? He said, he said that it – that it was him. That he was the one who deleted all of her emails, the 30,000 emails, because they basically dealt with her scheduling and her going to the gym and her having

beauty appointments. And he was great. And he, so she didn't get
in any trouble because he said that he was the one who deleted them.

TRUMP related the story more than once that day.

56.   On May 23, **TRUMP** also confirmed his understanding with Trump Attorney 1 that Trump Attorney 1 would return to The Mar-a-Lago Club on June 2 to search for any documents with classification markings to produce in response to the May 11 Subpoena. Trump Attorney 1 made it clear to **TRUMP** that Trump Attorney 1 would conduct the search for responsive documents by looking through **TRUMP**'s boxes that had been transported from the White House and remained in storage at The Mar-a-Lago Club. **TRUMP** indicated that he wanted to be at The Mar-a-Lago Club when Trump Attorney 1 returned to review his boxes on June 2, and that **TRUMP** would change his summer travel plans to do so. **TRUMP** told Trump Attorney 2 that Trump Attorney 2 did not need to be present for the review of boxes.

57.   After meeting with Trump Attorney 1 and Trump Attorney 2 on May 23, **TRUMP** delayed his departure from The Mar-a-Lago Club to The Bedminster Club for the summer so that he would be present at The Mar-a-Lago Club on June 2, when Trump Attorney 1 returned to review the boxes.

58.   Between **TRUMP**'s May 23 meeting with Trump Attorney 1 and Trump Attorney 2 to discuss the May 11 Subpoena, and June 2, when Trump Attorney 1 returned to The Mar-a-Lago Club to review the boxes in the Storage Room, **NAUTA** removed—at **TRUMP**'s direction—a total of approximately 64 boxes from the Storage Room and brought them to **TRUMP**'s residence, as set forth below:

    a.   On May 24, 2022, between 5:30 p.m. and 5:38 p.m., **NAUTA** removed three boxes from the Storage Room.

b. On May 30, 2022, at 9:08 a.m., **TRUMP** and **NAUTA** spoke by phone for approximately 30 seconds. Between 10:02 a.m. and 11:51 a.m., **NAUTA** removed a total of approximately 50 boxes from the Storage Room.

c. On May 30, 2022, at 12:33 p.m., a Trump family member texted **NAUTA**:

> Good afternoon Walt,
> Happy Memorial Day!
>
> I saw you put boxes to Potus room. Just FYI and I will tell him as well:
> Not sure how many he wants to take on Friday on the plane. We will NOT have a room for them. Plane will be full with luggage.
> Thank you!

NAUTA replied:

> Good Afternoon Ma'am [Smiley Face Emoji]
> Thank you so much.
>
> I think he wanted to pick from them. I don't imagine him wanting to take the boxes.
>
> He told me to put them in the room and that he was going to talk to you about them.

d. On June 1, 2022, beginning at 12:52 p.m., **NAUTA** removed approximately 11 boxes from the Storage Room.

59. On June 1, 2022, **TRUMP** spoke with Trump Attorney 1 by phone and asked whether Trump Attorney 1 was coming to The Mar-a-Lago Club the next day and for exactly what purpose. Trump Attorney 1 reminded **TRUMP** that Trump Attorney 1 was going to review the boxes that had been transported from the White House and remained in storage at The Mar-a-Lago Club so that Trump Attorney 1 could have a custodian of records certify that the May 11 subpoena had been complied with fully.

60.   On June 2, 2022, the day that Trump Attorney 1 was scheduled to review **TRUMP**'s boxes in the Storage Room, **TRUMP** spoke with **NAUTA** on the phone at 9:29 a.m. for approximately 24 seconds.

61.   Later that day, between 12:33 p.m. and 12:52 p.m., **NAUTA** and an employee of The Mar-a-Lago Club moved approximately 30 boxes from **TRUMP**'s residence to the Storage Room.

62.   In sum, between May 23, 2022, and June 2, 2022, before Trump Attorney 1's review of **TRUMP**'s boxes in the Storage Room, **NAUTA**—at **TRUMP**'s direction—moved approximately 64 boxes from the Storage Room to **TRUMP**'s residence and brought to the Storage Room only approximately 30 boxes. Neither **TRUMP** nor **NAUTA** informed Trump Attorney 1 of this information.

The False Certification to the FBI and the Grand Jury

63.   On the afternoon of June 2, 2022, as **TRUMP** had been informed, Trump Attorney 1 arrived at The Mar-a-Lago Club to review **TRUMP**'s boxes to look for documents with classification markings in response to the May 11 Subpoena. **TRUMP** met with Trump Attorney 1 before Trump Attorney 1 conducted the review. **NAUTA** escorted Trump Attorney 1 to the Storage Room.

64.   Between 3:53 p.m. and 6:23 p.m., Trump Attorney 1 reviewed the contents of **TRUMP**'s boxes in the Storage Room. Trump Attorney 1 located 38 documents with classification markings inside the boxes, which Trump Attorney 1 removed and placed in a Redweld folder. Trump Attorney 1 contacted **NAUTA** and asked him to bring clear duct tape to the Storage Room, which **NAUTA** did. Trump Attorney 1 used the clear duct tape to seal the Redweld folder with the documents with classification markings inside.

65.   After Trump Attorney 1 finished sealing the Redweld folder containing the documents with classification markings that he had found inside **TRUMP**'s boxes, **NAUTA** took Trump Attorney 1 to a dining room in The Mar-a-Lago Club to meet with **TRUMP**. After Trump Attorney 1 confirmed that he was finished with his search of the Storage Room, **TRUMP** asked, "Did you find anything? . . . Is it bad? Good?"

66.   **TRUMP** and Trump Attorney 1 then discussed what to do with the Redweld folder containing documents with classification markings and whether Trump Attorney 1 should bring them to his hotel room and put them in a safe there. During that conversation, **TRUMP** made a plucking motion, as memorialized by Trump Attorney 1:

> He made a funny motion as though – well okay why don't you take
> them with you to your hotel room and if there's anything really bad
> in there, like, you know, pluck it out. And that was the motion that
> he made. He didn't say that.

67.   That evening, Trump Attorney 1 contacted the Department of Justice and requested that an FBI agent meet him at The Mar-a-Lago Club the next day, June 3, so that he could turn over the documents responsive to the May 11 Subpoena.

68.   Also that evening, Trump Attorney 1 contacted another **TRUMP** attorney ("Trump Attorney 3") and asked her if she would come to The Mar-a-Lago Club the next morning to act as a custodian of records and sign a certification regarding the search for documents with classification markings in response to the May 11 Subpoena. Trump Attorney 3, who had no role in the review of **TRUMP**'s boxes in the Storage Room, agreed.

69.   The next day, on June 3, 2022, at Trump Attorney 1's request, Trump Attorney 3 signed a certification as the custodian of records for The Office of Donald J. Trump and took it to The Mar-a-Lago Club to provide it to the Department of Justice and FBI. In the certification, Trump Attorney 3—who performed no search of **TRUMP**'s boxes, had not reviewed the May 11

Subpoena, and had not reviewed the contents of the Redweld folder—stated, among other things, that "[b]ased upon the information that [had] been provided to" her:

a. "A diligent search was conducted of the boxes that were moved from the White House to Florida";

b. "This search was conducted after receipt of the subpoena, in order to locate any and all documents that are responsive to the subpoena"; and

c. "Any and all responsive documents accompany this certification."

70.   These statements were false because, among other reasons, **TRUMP** had directed **NAUTA** to move boxes before Trump Attorney 1's June 2 review, so that many boxes were not searched and many documents responsive to the May 11 Subpoena could not be found—and in fact were not found—by Trump Attorney 1.

71.   Shortly after Trump Attorney 3 executed the false certification, on June 3, 2022, Trump Attorney 1 and Trump Attorney 3 met at The Mar-a-Lago Club with personnel from the Department of Justice and FBI. Trump Attorney 1 and Trump Attorney 3 turned over the Redweld folder containing documents with classification markings, as well as the false certification signed by Trump Attorney 3 as custodian of records. **TRUMP**, who had delayed his departure from The Mar-a-Lago Club, joined Trump Attorney 1 and Trump Attorney 3 for some of the meeting. **TRUMP** claimed to the Department of Justice and FBI that he was "an open book."

72.   Earlier that same day, **NAUTA** and others loaded several of **TRUMP**'s boxes along with other items on aircraft that flew **TRUMP** and his family north for the summer.

The Court-Authorized Search of The Mar-a-Lago Club

73.   In July 2022, the FBI and grand jury obtained and reviewed surveillance video from The Mar-a-Lago Club showing the movement of boxes set forth above.

74.   On August 8, 2022, the FBI executed a court-authorized search warrant at The Mar-a-Lago Club. The search warrant authorized the FBI to search for and seize, among other things, all documents with classification markings.

75.   During the execution of the warrant at The Mar-a-Lago Club, the FBI seized 102 documents with classification markings in **TRUMP**'s office and the Storage Room, as follows:

Location	Number of Documents	Classification Markings
TRUMP's Office	27	Top Secret (6) Secret (18) Confidential (3)
Storage Room	75	Top Secret (11) Secret (36) Confidential (28)

COUNTS 1-31
Willful Retention of National Defense Information
(18 U.S.C. § 793(e))

76.   The General Allegations of this Indictment are re-alleged and fully incorporated here by reference.

77.   On or about the dates set forth in the table below, in Palm Beach County, in the Southern District of Florida, and elsewhere, the defendant,

DONALD J. TRUMP,

having unauthorized possession of, access to, and control over documents relating to the national defense, did willfully retain the documents and fail to deliver them to the officer and employee of the United States entitled to receive them; that is—**TRUMP**, without authorization, retained at The Mar-a-Lago Club documents relating to the national defense, including the following:

Count	Date of Offense / Classification Marking / Document Description
1	January 20, 2021 – August 8, 2022
	TOP SECRET//NOFORN//SPECIAL HANDLING
	Document dated May 3, 2018, concerning White House intelligence briefing related to various foreign countries
2	January 20, 2021 – August 8, 2022
	TOP SECRET//SI//NOFORN//SPECIAL HANDLING
	Document dated May 9, 2018, concerning White House intelligence briefing related to various foreign countries
3	January 20, 2021 – August 8, 2022
	TOP SECRET//SI//NOFORN//FISA
	Undated document concerning military capabilities of a foreign country and the United States, with handwritten annotation in black marker

4	January 20, 2021 – August 8, 2022
	TOP SECRET//SPECIAL HANDLING
	Document dated May 6, 2019, concerning White House intelligence briefing related to foreign countries, including military activities and planning of foreign countries
5	January 20, 2021 – August 8, 2022
	TOP SECRET//[redacted]/[redacted]//ORCON/NOFORN
	Document dated June 2020 concerning nuclear capabilities of a foreign country
6	January 20, 2021 – August 8, 2022
	TOP SECRET//SPECIAL HANDLING
	Document dated June 4, 2020, concerning White House intelligence briefing related to various foreign countries
7	January 20, 2021 – August 8, 2022
	SECRET//NOFORN
	Document dated October 21, 2018, concerning communications with a leader of a foreign country
8	January 20, 2021 – August 8, 2022
	SECRET//REL TO USA, FVEY
	Document dated October 4, 2019, concerning military capabilities of a foreign country
9	January 20, 2021 – August 8, 2022
	TOP SECRET//[redacted]/[redacted]//ORCON/NOFORN/FISA
	Undated document concerning military attacks by a foreign country

10	January 20, 2021 – August 8, 2022
	TOP SECRET//TK//NOFORN
	Document dated November 2017 concerning military capabilities of a foreign country
11	January 20, 2021 – August 8, 2022
	No marking
	Undated document concerning military contingency planning of the United States
12	January 20, 2021 – August 8, 2022
	SECRET//REL TO USA, FVEY
	Pages of undated document concerning projected regional military capabilities of a foreign country and the United States
13	January 20, 2021 – August 8, 2022
	TOP SECRET//SI/TK//NOFORN
	Undated document concerning military capabilities of a foreign country and the United States
14	January 20, 2021 – August 8, 2022
	SECRET//ORCON/NOFORN
	Document dated January 2020 concerning military options of a foreign country and potential effects on United States interests
15	January 20, 2021 – August 8, 2022
	SECRET//ORCON/NOFORN
	Document dated February 2020 concerning policies in a foreign country

16	January 20, 2021 – August 8, 2022
	SECRET//ORCON/NOFORN
	Document dated December 2019 concerning foreign country support of terrorist acts against United States interests
17	January 20, 2021 – August 8, 2022
	TOP SECRET//[redacted]/TK//ORCON/IMCON/NOFORN
	Document dated January 2020 concerning military capabilities of a foreign country
18	January 20, 2021 – August 8, 2022
	SECRET//NOFORN
	Document dated March 2020 concerning military operations against United States forces and others
19	January 20, 2021 – August 8, 2022
	SECRET//FORMERLY RESTRICTED DATA
	Undated document concerning nuclear weaponry of the United States
20	January 20, 2021 – August 8, 2022
	TOP SECRET//[redacted]//ORCON/NOFORN
	Undated document concerning timeline and details of attack in a foreign country
21	January 20, 2021 – August 8, 2022
	SECRET//NOFORN
	Undated document concerning military capabilities of foreign countries
22	January 20, 2021 – June 3, 2022
	TOP SECRET//[redacted]//RSEN/ORCON/NOFORN
	Document dated August 2019 concerning regional military activity of a foreign country

23	January 20, 2021 – June 3, 2022
	TOP SECRET//SPECIAL HANDLING
	Document dated August 30, 2019, concerning White House intelligence briefing related to various foreign countries, with handwritten annotation in black marker
24	January 20, 2021 – June 3, 2022
	TOP SECRET//HCS-P/SI//ORCON-USGOV/NOFORN
	Undated document concerning military activity of a foreign country
25	January 20, 2021 – June 3, 2022
	TOP SECRET//HCS-P/SI//ORCON-USGOV/NOFORN
	Document dated October 24, 2019, concerning military activity of foreign countries and the United States
26	January 20, 2021 – June 3, 2022
	TOP SECRET//[redacted]//ORCON/NOFORN/FISA
	Document dated November 7, 2019, concerning military activity of foreign countries and the United States
27	January 20, 2021 – June 3, 2022
	TOP SECRET//SI/TK//NOFORN
	Document dated November 2019 concerning military activity of foreign countries
28	January 20, 2021 – June 3, 2022
	TOP SECRET//SPECIAL HANDLING
	Document dated October 18, 2019, concerning White House intelligence briefing related to various foreign countries

29	January 20, 2021 – June 3, 2022	
	TOP SECRET//[redacted]/SI/TK//ORCON/NOFORN	
	Document dated October 18, 2019, concerning military capabilities of a foreign country	
30	January 20, 2021 – June 3, 2022	
	TOP SECRET//[redacted]//ORCON/NOFORN/FISA	
	Document dated October 15, 2019, concerning military activity in a foreign country	
31	January 20, 2021 – June 3, 2022	
	TOP SECRET//SI/TK//NOFORN	
	Document dated February 2017 concerning military activity of a foreign country	

All in violation of Title 18, United States Code, Section 793(e).

COUNT 32
Conspiracy to Obstruct Justice
(18 U.S.C. § 1512(k))

78.   The General Allegations of this Indictment are re-alleged and fully incorporated here by reference.

The Conspiracy and its Objects

79.   From on or about May 11, 2022, through in or around August 2022, in Palm Beach County, in the Southern District of Florida, and elsewhere, the defendants,

DONALD J. TRUMP and
WALTINE NAUTA,

did knowingly combine, conspire, confederate, and agree with each other and with others known and unknown to the grand jury, to engage in misleading conduct toward another person and corruptly persuade another person to withhold a record, document, and other object from an official proceeding, in violation of 18 U.S.C. § 1512(b)(2)(A), and to corruptly conceal a record, document, and other object from an official proceeding, in violation of 18 U.S.C. § 1512(c)(1).

The Purpose of the Conspiracy

80.   The purpose of the conspiracy was for **TRUMP** to keep classified documents he had taken with him from the White House and to hide and conceal them from a federal grand jury.

The Manner and Means of the Conspiracy

81.   The manner and means by which the defendants sought to accomplish the objects and purpose of the conspiracy included, among other things, the following:

    a.   Suggesting that Trump Attorney 1 falsely represent to the FBI and grand jury that **TRUMP** did not have documents called for by the May 11 Subpoena;

    b.   moving boxes of documents to conceal them from Trump Attorney 1, the FBI, and the grand jury;

c. suggesting that Trump Attorney 1 hide or destroy documents called for by the May 11 Subpoena;

d. providing to the FBI and grand jury just some of the documents called for by the May 11 Subpoena, while **TRUMP** claimed he was cooperating fully;

e. causing a false certification to be submitted to the FBI and grand jury representing that all documents with classification markings had been produced, when in fact they had not; and

f. making false and misleading statements to the FBI.

All in violation of Title 18, United States Code, Section 1512(k).

COUNT 33
Withholding a Document or Record
(18 U.S.C. §§ 1512(b)(2)(A), 2)

82.   The General Allegations of this Indictment are re-alleged and fully incorporated here by reference.

83.   From on or about May 11, 2022, through in or around August 2022, in Palm Beach County, in the Southern District of Florida, and elsewhere, the defendants,

DONALD J. TRUMP and
WALTINE NAUTA,

did knowingly engage in misleading conduct toward another person, and knowingly corruptly persuade and attempt to persuade another person, with intent to cause and induce any person to withhold a record, document, and other object from an official proceeding; that is—(1) **TRUMP** attempted to persuade Trump Attorney 1 to hide and conceal documents from a federal grand jury; and (2) **TRUMP** and **NAUTA** misled Trump Attorney 1 by moving boxes that contained documents with classification markings so that Trump Attorney 1 would not find the documents and produce them to a federal grand jury.

All in violation of Title 18, United States Code, Sections 1512(b)(2)(A) and 2.

Corruptly Concealing a Document or Record
(18 U.S.C. §§ 1512(c)(1), 2)

84.   The General Allegations of this Indictment are re-alleged and fully incorporated here by reference.

85.   From on or about May 11, 2022, through in or around August 2022, in Palm Beach County, in the Southern District of Florida, and elsewhere, the defendants,

DONALD J. TRUMP and
WALTINE NAUTA,

did corruptly conceal a record, document, and other object, and attempted to do so, with the intent to impair the object's integrity and availability for use in an official proceeding; that is—**TRUMP** and **NAUTA** hid and concealed boxes that contained documents with classification markings from Trump Attorney 1 so that Trump Attorney 1 would not find the documents and produce them to a federal grand jury.

All in violation of Title 18, United States Code, Sections 1512(c)(1) and 2.

COUNT 35
Concealing a Document in a Federal Investigation
(18 U.S.C. §§ 1519, 2)

86.   The General Allegations of this Indictment are re-alleged and fully incorporated here by reference.

87.   From on or about May 11, 2022, through in or around August 2022, in Palm Beach County, in the Southern District of Florida, and elsewhere, the defendants,

DONALD J. TRUMP and
WALTINE NAUTA,

did knowingly conceal, cover up, falsify, and make a false entry in any record, document, and tangible object with the intent to impede, obstruct, and influence the investigation and proper administration of any matter within the jurisdiction of a department and agency of the United States, and in relation to and contemplation of any such matter; that is—during a federal criminal investigation being conducted by the FBI, (1) **TRUMP** and **NAUTA** hid, concealed, and covered up from the FBI **TRUMP**'s continued possession of documents with classification markings at The Mar-a-Lago Club; and (2) **TRUMP** caused a false certification to be submitted to the FBI.

All in violation of Title 18, United States Code, Sections 1519 and 2.

COUNT 36
Scheme to Conceal
(18 U.S.C. §§ 1001(a)(1), 2)

88.   The General Allegations of this Indictment are re-alleged and fully incorporated here by reference.

89.   From on or about May 11, 2022, through in or around August 2022, in Palm Beach County, in the Southern District of Florida, and elsewhere, the defendants,

DONALD J. TRUMP and
WALTINE NAUTA,

in a matter within the jurisdiction of the judicial branch and executive branch of the United States government, did knowingly and willfully falsify, conceal, and cover up by any trick, scheme, and device a material fact; that is—during a federal grand jury investigation and a federal criminal investigation being conducted by the FBI, **TRUMP** and **NAUTA** hid and concealed from the grand jury and the FBI **TRUMP**'s continued possession of documents with classification markings.

All in violation of Title 18, United States Code, Sections 1001(a)(1) and 2.

COUNT 37
False Statements and Representations
(18 U.S.C. §§ 1001(a)(2), 2)

90.   The General Allegations of this Indictment are re-alleged and fully incorporated here by reference.

91.   On or about June 3, 2022, in Palm Beach County, in the Southern District of Florida, and elsewhere, the defendant,

DONALD J. TRUMP,

in a matter within the jurisdiction of the judicial branch and executive branch of the United States government, did knowingly and willfully make and cause to be made a materially false, fictitious, and fraudulent statement and representation; that is—during a federal grand jury investigation and a federal criminal investigation being conducted by the FBI, **TRUMP** caused the following false statements and representations to be made to the grand jury and the FBI in a sworn certification executed by Trump Attorney 3:

   a.   "A diligent search was conducted of the boxes that were moved from the White House to Florida";

   b.   "This search was conducted after receipt of the subpoena, in order to locate any and all documents that are responsive to the subpoena"; and

   c.   "Any and all responsive documents accompany this certification."

92.   The statements and representations set forth above were false, as **TRUMP** knew, because **TRUMP** had directed that boxes be removed from the Storage Room before Trump Attorney 1 conducted the June 2, 2022 search for documents with classification markings, so that Trump Attorney 1's search would not and did not include all of **TRUMP**'s boxes that were removed from the White House; Trump Attorney 1's search would not and did not locate all

documents responsive to the May 11 Subpoena; and all responsive documents were not provided to the FBI and the grand jury with the certification. In fact, after June 3, 2022, more than 100 documents with classification markings remained at The Mar-a-Lago Club until the FBI search on August 8, 2022.

All in violation of Title 18, United States Code, Sections 1001(a)(2) and 2.

COUNT 38
False Statements and Representations
(18 U.S.C. § 1001(a)(2))

93.   The General Allegations of this Indictment are re-alleged and fully incorporated here by reference.

94.   On May 26, 2022, **NAUTA** participated in a voluntary interview with the FBI. During the interview, the FBI explained to **NAUTA** that the FBI was investigating how classified documents had been kept at The Mar-a-Lago Club, and the FBI asked **NAUTA** questions about the location and movement of **TRUMP**'s boxes before **TRUMP** provided 15 boxes to NARA on January 17, 2022. **NAUTA** was represented by counsel, and the FBI advised **NAUTA** that the interview was voluntary and that he could leave at any time. The FBI also advised **NAUTA** that it was a criminal offense to lie to the FBI. The interview was recorded.

95.   On or about May 26, 2022, in Palm Beach County, in the Southern District of Florida, and elsewhere, the defendant,

WALTINE NAUTA,

in a matter within the jurisdiction of the executive branch of the United States government, did knowingly and willfully make a materially false, fictitious, and fraudulent statement and representation; that is—in a voluntary interview during a federal criminal investigation being conducted by the FBI, **NAUTA** was asked the following questions and gave the following false answers:

Question: Does any – are you aware of any boxes being brought to his home – his suite?

Answer: **No.**

* * *

Question: All right. So, so to the best of your knowledge, you're saying that those boxes that you brought onto the truck, first time you ever laid eyes on them was just the day of when [Trump Employee 2] needed you to—

Answer: **Correct.**

Question: —to take them. Okay.

* * *

Question: In knowing that we're trying to track the life of these boxes and where they could have been kept and stored and all that kind of stuff—

Answer: Mm-hm.

Question: —do you have any information that could—that would—that could help us understand, like, where they were kept, how they were kept, were they secured, were they locked? Something that makes the intelligence community feel better about these things, you know?

Answer: **I wish, I wish I could tell you. I don't know. I don't—I honestly just don't know.**

* * *

Question: And what—so, so you only saw the 15 boxes, 15, 17 boxes—

Answer: Mm-hm.

Question: —the day of the move? Even—they just showed up that day?

Answer: They were in Pine Hall. [Trump Employee 2] just asked me, hey, can we move some boxes?

Question: Okay.

Answer: And I was like, okay.

Question:	So, you didn't know—had no idea how they got there before?
Answer:	**No.**

96.   The underscored statements and representations above were false, as **NAUTA** knew, because (1) **NAUTA** did in fact know that the boxes in Pine Hall had come from the Storage Room, as **NAUTA** himself, with the assistance of Trump Employee 2, had moved the boxes from the Storage Room to Pine Hall; and (2) **NAUTA** had observed the boxes in and moved them to various locations at The Mar-a-Lago Club.

All in violation of Title 18, United States Code, Section 1001(a)(2).

A TRUE BILL

_____
FOREPERSON

_____
JACK SMITH
SPECIAL COUNSEL
UNITED STATES DEPARTMENT OF JUSTICE

UNITED STATES DISTRICT COURT
SOUTHERN DISTRICT OF FLORIDA

UNITED STATES OF AMERICA

CASE NO.: _____

v.

Donald J. Trump and
Waltine Nauta,
_____ /
Defendants.

CERTIFICATE OF TRIAL ATTORNEY

Superseding Case Information:
New Defendant(s) (Yes or No) No
Number of New Defendants _____
Total number of counts _____

Court Division (select one)
☐ Miami ☐ Key West ☐ FTP
☐ FTL ☒ WPB

I do hereby certify that:

1. I have carefully considered the allegations of the indictment, the number of defendants, the number of probable witnesses and the legal complexities of the Indictment/Information attached hereto.

2. I am aware that the information supplied on this statement will be relied upon by the Judges of this Court in setting their calendars and scheduling criminal trials under the mandate of the Speedy Trial Act, Title 28 U.S.C. §3161.

3. Interpreter: (Yes or No) No
   List language and/or dialect: _____

4. This case will take __21__ days for the parties to try.

5. Please check appropriate category and type of offense listed below:

   (Check only one)   (Check only one)
   I   ☐ 0 to 5 days   ☐ Petty
   II   ☐ 6 to 10 days   ☐ Minor
   III ☐ 11 to 20 days   ☐ Misdemeanor
   IV   ☒ 21 to 60 days   ☒ Felony
   V   ☐ 61 days and over

6. Has this case been previously filed in this District Court? (Yes or No) No
   If yes, Judge _____ Case No. _____

7. Has a complaint been filed in this matter? (Yes or No) No
   If yes, Magistrate Case No. _____

8. Does this case relate to a previously filed matter in this District Court? (Yes or No) No
   If yes, Judge _____ Case No. _____

9. Defendant(s) in federal custody as of _____

10. Defendant(s) in state custody as of _____

11. Rule 20 from the _____ District of _____

12. Is this a potential death penalty case? (Yes or No) No

13. Does this case originate from a matter pending in the Northern Region of the U.S. Attorney's Office prior to August 8, 2014 (Mag. Judge Shaniek Maynard? (Yes or No) No

14. Does this case originate from a matter pending in the Central Region of the U.S. Attorney's Office prior to October 3, 2019 (Mag. Judge Jared Strauss? (Yes or No) No

15. Did this matter involve the participation of or consultation with now Magistrate Judge Eduardo I. Sanchez during his tenure at the U.S. Attorney's Office, which concluded on January 22, 2023? No

By: _____
Jay I. Bratt
Assistant Special Counsel
Court ID No. A5502946

UNITED STATES DISTRICT COURT
SOUTHERN DISTRICT OF FLORIDA

PENALTY SHEET

Defendant's Name: Donald J. Trump

Case No: _____

Counts #: 1-31

Willful Retention of National Defense Information, 18 U.S.C. § 793(e)

* **Max. Term of Imprisonment: 10 years**
* **Mandatory Min. Term of Imprisonment (if applicable): N/A**
* **Max. Supervised Release: 3 years**
* **Max. Fine: $250,000**

Count #: 32

Conspiracy to Obstruct Justice, 18 U.S.C. § 1512(k)

* **Max. Term of Imprisonment: 20 years**
* **Mandatory Min. Term of Imprisonment (if applicable): N/A**
* **Max. Supervised Release: 3 years**
* **Max. Fine: $250,000**

Count #: 33

Withholding a Document or Record, 18 U.S.C. § 1512(b)(2)(A)

* **Max. Term of Imprisonment: 20 years**
* **Mandatory Min. Term of Imprisonment (if applicable): N/A**
* **Max. Supervised Release: 3 years**
* **Max. Fine: $250,000**

*Refers only to possible term of incarceration, supervised release and fines.   It does not include restitution, special assessments, parole terms, or forfeitures that may be applicable.

Count #: 34

Corruptly Concealing a Document or Record, 18 U.S.C. § 1512(c)(1)

* **Max. Term of Imprisonment: 20 years**
* **Mandatory Min. Term of Imprisonment (if applicable): N/A**
* **Max. Supervised Release: 3 years**
* **Max. Fine: $250,000**

Count #: 35

Concealing a Document in a Federal Investigation, 18 U.S.C. § 1519

* **Max. Term of Imprisonment: 20 years**
* **Mandatory Min. Term of Imprisonment (if applicable): N/A**
* **Max. Supervised Release: 3 years**
* **Max. Fine: $250,000**

Count #: 36

Scheme to Conceal, 18 U.S.C. § 1001(a)(1)

* **Max. Term of Imprisonment: 5 years**
* **Mandatory Min. Term of Imprisonment (if applicable): N/A**
* **Max. Supervised Release: 3 years**
* **Max. Fine: $250,000**

Count #: 37

False Statements and Representations, 18 U.S.C. § 1001(a)(2)

* **Max. Term of Imprisonment: 5 years**
* **Mandatory Min. Term of Imprisonment (if applicable): N/A**
* **Max. Supervised Release: 3 years**
* **Max. Fine: $250,000**

*Refers only to possible term of incarceration, supervised release and fines. It does not include restitution, special assessments, parole terms, or forfeitures that may be applicable.

UNITED STATES DISTRICT COURT
SOUTHERN DISTRICT OF FLORIDA

PENALTY SHEET

Defendant's Name: Waltine Nauta

Case No: _____

Count #: 32

Conspiracy to Obstruct Justice, 18 U.S.C. § 1512(k)

* Max. Term of Imprisonment: 20 years
* Mandatory Min. Term of Imprisonment (if applicable): N/A
* Max. Supervised Release: 3 years
* Max. Fine: $250,000

Count #: 33

Withholding a Document or Record, 18 U.S.C. § 1512(b)(2)(A)

* Max. Term of Imprisonment: 20 years
* Mandatory Min. Term of Imprisonment (if applicable): N/A
* Max. Supervised Release: 3 years
* Max. Fine: $250,000

Count #: 34

Corruptly Concealing a Document or Record, 18 U.S.C. § 1512(c)(1)

* Max. Term of Imprisonment: 20 years
* Mandatory Min. Term of Imprisonment (if applicable): N/A
* Max. Supervised Release: 3 years
* Max. Fine: $250,000

Count #: 35

Concealing a Document in a Federal Investigation, 18 U.S.C. § 1519

* Max. Term of Imprisonment: 20 years
* Mandatory Min. Term of Imprisonment (if applicable): N/A
* Max. Supervised Release: 3 years
* Max. Fine: $250,000

*Refers only to possible term of incarceration, supervised release and fines.   It does not include restitution, special assessments, parole terms, or forfeitures that may be applicable.

Count #: 36

Scheme to Conceal, 18 U.S.C. § 1001(a)(1)

* **Max. Term of Imprisonment: 5 years**
* **Mandatory Min. Term of Imprisonment (if applicable): N/A**
* **Max. Supervised Release: 3 years**
* **Max. Fine: $250,000**

Count #: 38

False Statements and Representations, 18 U.S.C. § 1001(a)(2)

* **Max. Term of Imprisonment: 5 years**
* **Mandatory Min. Term of Imprisonment (if applicable): N/A**
* **Max. Supervised Release: 3 years**
* **Max. Fine: $250,000**

*Refers only to possible term of incarceration, supervised release and fines. It does not include restitution, special assessments, parole terms, or forfeitures that may be applicable.

9 781566 494304